Plant Based Diet for Beginners

Revitalize Your Life, Take Control of Your Weight, and Enjoy Delicious Food

Amellia Fox

© **Copyright 2017 by Amellia Fox - All rights reserved.**

This document is geared towards providing exact and reliable information in regards to the topic and issue covered. The publication is sold with the idea that the publisher is not required to render accounting, officially permitted, or otherwise, qualified services. If advice is necessary, legal or professional, a practiced individual in the profession should be ordered.

- From a Declaration of Principles which was accepted and approved equally by a Committee of the American Bar Association and a Committee of Publishers and Associations.

In no way is it legal to reproduce, duplicate, or transmit any part of this document in either electronic means or in printed format. Recording of this publication is strictly prohibited and any storage of this document is not allowed unless with written permission from the publisher. All rights reserved.

The information provided herein is stated to be truthful and consistent, in that any liability, in terms of inattention or otherwise, by any usage or abuse of any policies, processes, or directions contained within is the solitary and utter responsibility of the recipient reader. Under no circumstances will any legal responsibility or blame be held against the publisher for any reparation, damages, or monetary loss due to the information herein, either directly or indirectly.

Respective authors own all copyrights not held by the publisher.

The information herein is offered for informational purposes solely, and is universal as so. The presentation of the information is without contract or any type of guarantee assurance.

The trademarks that are used are without any consent, and the publication of the trademark is without permission or backing by the trademark owner. All trademarks and brands within this book are for clarifying purposes only and are the owned by the owners themselves, not affiliated with this document.

Table of Contents

Introduction - Making a Positive Change 4

Chapter 1 – The Basics 6
- What is a plant-based diet?
- Types of plant-based diets

Chapter 2 – Getting Started 9
- The top 10 MVPs of a plant-based diet
- Gradually incorporating plant-based foods into your diet

Chapter 3 – The Benefits 21
- Combatting diseases and health conditions
- Mental health and sleep
- Youthful skin

Chapter 4 – Weight Loss 26
- Sustainable results

Chapter 5 – Concerns 29
- Will I get enough protein and iron?

Chapter 6 – Easy, Delicious Recipes 32
- Breakfast, lunch, dinner and snacks!

Conclusion 44

Introduction - Making a Positive Change

Are you utterly fed up with feeling fatigued, unmotivated, and unhealthy? Are you looking for a lifestyle change that will help you stop overeating, give you more energy, and improve your quality of life? A plant-based diet will provide just the kind of change you are looking for. Millions of people across the world have made the shift to eating food sourced from plants and you can too. Embarking upon a plant-based diet is a lot easier than it may seem. We have been told by society that meat and animal products are a necessity and we absolutely cannot do without them, but that is just evidently false. There are countless people living healthy, fulfilling, thriving lives who subscribe to plant-based diets and who would certainly beg to differ. A plant-based diet offers you freedom from the cycle of eating unhealthy processed foods, eases your environmental and humane conscious, and all together promotes better health and living.

There are so many unhealthy food choices out there in our world today and in our busy, fast-paced culture, eating healthy often takes a backseat. We reach for options like junk food and other heavily processed products that cause us to gain weight that is hard to lose and makes us sluggish and unmotivated because they are so readily available. Who has the time to carefully curate their meals when there are such easy, albeit extremely unhealthy, options like fast-food, microwavable meals, and addictive, cheap food products so readily available wherever we go in major supermarkets and restaurants? These foods satisfy our cravings and give us a false sense of satisfaction, but in reality, they deplete our energy and send us into a vicious cycle of overeating and unhealthy choices. So many of us today are affected by weight and health issues because we are not eating properly. It is difficult to resist temptation, however, when we are constantly being targeted by deceptive food companies marketing products that fill us up and give us the illusion of gratification. The momentary comfort and enjoyment of indulging in unhealthy foods are far outweighed by the detrimental effects they have on our health. Foods high in saturated fat, sugar, and harsh preservative chemicals slow us down, make us feel worse, and cause a multitude of dangerous health problems. It is no wonder that many people are deciding to break free from the cycle of unhealthy eating and choosing to follow a healthier, more fulfilling lifestyle.

So many healthy, nutritious options exist and are out there for those looking to make a change. However, understandably, for a novice entering the realm of healthy eating and living, it can definitely feel overwhelming. There are so many different diet options, it is hard to know which one to try and which one will work best for you. For people seeking to lose weight, there are also countless dangerous fad diets out there that may help you lose a few pounds quickly but are not sustainable or healthy in the long-run. A plant-based diet is one of the healthiest and safest options out there. Countless people have made the change and are living healthier, more balanced, and well-rounded lives because of it. It is proven to help you lose and keep off weight, reduce your risk for many diseases, promote energy, and improve overall well-being. But how do you start? Changing the way you eat is a monumental and pivotal lifestyle change. You have to learn and reinforce new habits, have self-discipline, and a good deal of commitment. It can seem like an impossible task it you do not know where to begin.

That's where this beginners guide comes in! Switching to a plant-based diet and eating healthy does not have to be difficult or daunting. All you need is a little motivation and the desire to make a positive change. There are many ways to make the change successfully that do not involve breaking your bank account, stressing out about what you can or cannot eat, or finding yourself lost in a sea of timely meal prep. Eating healthy does not have to be a chore or a burden! In this guide for beginners seeking to make the positive lifestyle change to a yummy, healthy, and easy plant-based diet, you will learn exactly what a plant-based diet entails, how to make easy, fulfilling meals that give you all the nutrients you need, and smoothly transition into a healthier and rewarding diet. Are you willing to make the change and give yourself the healthier, more fulfilled life you deserve? Are you ready to revitalize your life, take control of your weight, and enjoy delicious food? If so, read on!

CHAPTER 1 – The Basics

So, first things first, what is a plant-based diet? We hear this term thrown around quite a lot and so there may be some confusion as to what a plant-based diet actually entails. The truth is, there is no one catch-all answer to this question, as a plant-based diet can take on many different forms and variations. The general consensus is that a plant-based diet involves large amounts of plant products, whole foods and limited amounts of animal products and processed foods. However, subscribing to a plant-based diet does not necessarily mean that you have to cut out all forms of meat and animal products. You can tailor your diet to fit your needs and lifestyle. Many people who have shifted to a plant-based diet recommend a gradual transition in which you slowly cut out animal products from your meals. This will allow you to see what works for you and help you decide what variation of a plant-based diet is right for you.

Though there are variations within a plant-based diet, the major cornerstone of the diet is that plant foods become the central focal point of your diet. This means that you base your meals around food products sourced from plants like vegetables, nuts, seeds, whole grains, fruits, and legumes. Animal products are either cut out completely or are otherwise reduced. How much you reduce your intake of animal products depends upon what you deem best for yourself. However, if you do choose to make animal products such as fish, poultry, meat, dairy, or eggs a part of your diet, they will take a backseat to the plant foods that make up your meals. If this makes you feel nervous, don't worry! This is not a deprivation diet. There are so many appetizing and tasty plant food options out there that you may not even know about! Many of us are so accustomed to meat, animal products and processed foods taking center-stage at meal times that it is hard to imagine what a meal that puts plant foods first would look like. Embarking on a plant-based diet provides you an exciting opportunity to explore new foods and recipes that are not only satisfying and nourishing but are delicious and taste amazing as well.

The following diets all fall under the umbrella of a plant-based diet.

- **Vegan**: Diet includes vegetables, seeds, nuts, legumes, grains, and fruit and excludes all animal products (i.e. no animal flesh, dairy, or eggs). There are variations within the vegan diet as well such as the **fruitarian** diet made up mainly of fruits and sometimes nuts and seeds and the **raw vegan** diet where food is not cooked.

- **Vegetarian**: Diet includes vegetables, fruit, nuts, legumes, grains, and seeds and excludes meat but may include eggs or dairy. The **Ovo-lacto vegetarian** diet incorporates dairy and eggs while the **Ovo-vegetarian** diet incorporates eggs and excludes dairy and the **lacto vegetarian** diet incorporates dairy but excludes eggs.

- **Semi-vegetarianism:** Diet is mostly vegetarian but also incorporates some meat and animal products. The **macrobiotic** diet is a type of semi-vegetarian diet that emphasizes vegetables, beans, whole grains, naturally processed foods, and may include some seafood, meat, or poultry. The **pescatarian** diet includes plant foods, eggs, dairy, and seafood but no other types of animal flesh. People who subscribe to a semi-vegetarian diet sometimes describe themselves as flexitarians as well.

The plant-based, whole food diet is really all about trying to only consume whole, unrefined plants. Followers of a plant-based diet like to get their food as organically as possible. If the food is refined, it must only be minimally refined. Vegetables, fruits, whole grains, tubers, and legumes are going to be the most important parts of meals and animal products either take a on a small proportion of the meal or are excluded altogether. This includes meat, dairy products, and eggs. Highly refined products like bleached flour, oil, and refined sugar are usually avoided as well.

Some of these plant-based diets are obviously stricter than others. No one diet is right for everyone, so it is important to understand all the options you have within a plant-based diet so that you can choose which lifestyle is most attractive and feels right to you. Maybe you want to cut out all animal products and go vegan, consuming only plant foods and products or maybe you prefer keeping some animal products in your diet while making plant foods your main focus. Remember, you are in control of what you eat and what goes into your body. A plant-based diet will likely have more restrictions and parameters than you are used to, so it is crucial that you pick a diet that is not only healthy, but attainable, realistic to adhere to, and enjoyable for you. The plant-based diet is designed to increase your quality of life so it would be counter-productive to choose a diet that makes you feel deprived or unhappy! It is important to set realistic expectations for yourself so that you are able to follow your new diet and are not tempted to stray from it. That being said, following a plant-based diet can be incredibly easy and simple if you follow the right steps and stay committed to your new healthy choices which will not be hard to do once you start feeling the beneficial effects of this health-focused lifestyle.

CHAPTER 2 – Getting Started

The first thing to be sure of when starting a plant-based diet is that you know what plant foods are going to get you the best bang for your buck. There are a lot of great options out there, but honing in on the most potent (those foods containing the most vitamins, minerals, and nutrients) will really maximize the benefits you are looking to get out of a plant-based diet. So, go for gold and choose the foods that will really make your meals worthwhile. These foods will be like the MVPs (Most Valuable Players) of your new diet. They will help you get the most out of a plant-based diet, make you healthier, and ensure that your food intake is balanced and wholesome. Here are a few Top Ten MVP lists you should keep in mind when planning your plant-based meals:

Vegetables and Legumes

1. Edamame

    These cooked soybeans are not only delicious, they also have an incredible amount of protein. In just one cup, a serving of edamame will give you 18 grams of protein. Look for the certified organic seal, though, because many soybeans in the United States are treated with pesticides or genetically modified. Edamame works great as a stand-alone snack or appetizer and can also be added into meals as a side or in a stir-fry.

2. Lentils

    Easy to incorporate into almost any meal in a variety of forms, lentils provide an excellent source of low-calorie and high-fiber protein. They contain 9 grams of protein per half cup serving. They are also incredibly helpful in lowering cholesterol and promoting heart health. You can prepare them as a side dish, use them to make veggie burgers, substitute them for meat and make a delicious taco filling in a slow cooker or make a yummy dip with them.

3. Black Beans
   Black beans are another vegetable like lentils that are wonderfully multi-use. They have great fiber, folate, potassium, and vitamin B6. They contain 7.6 grams of protein in every serving and can be used to make anything from veggie burgers to vegan brownies. Imagine that!

4. Potatoes
   Potatoes are a great, low-cost source of protein (4 grams per medium potato) and potassium. They're tasty and heart-healthy!

5. Spinach
   One of the best green vegetables for protein (3 grams per serving), cooked spinach is an excellent addition to your plant-based diet.

6. Broccoli
   When cooked, you get 2 grams per serving of this vegetable and also an excellent dose of fiber.

7. Brussels Sprouts
   Another great green vegetable for protein, brussels sprouts gives you 2 grams of protein per serving alongside a great deal of potassium and vitamin K. Be sure to get the fresh version, though, as they taste a whole lot better than the frozen kind!

8. Lima Beans
   Containing 7.3 grams of protein per serving when cooked, lima beans make an amazing side dish or addition to a healthy salad. They also contain leucine, an amino acid that aids in muscle synthesis!

9. Peanuts and Peanut Butter
   Widely recognized as a superfood by meat-eaters and plant-based eaters alike, peanuts and peanut butter contain 7 grams of protein per serving and can be

used in so many different ways. And who doesn't love a good childhood staple PB&J sandwich? Nearly all kinds of peanut butter are vegan, but keep a lookout for any that might contain honey if you are keeping strictly vegan and cutting out all animal products.

10. Chickpeas

    Chickpeas are another versatile legume that can be prepared in a multitude of ways. Perhaps the most popular preparation is in the form of delicious hummus. With 6 grams of protein per serving, it'll be hard not to spread it on everything you eat!

Nuts and Seeds

1. Chia Seeds

   Chia seeds are amazing sources of vitamin C, protein, fiber, and calcium. They have to be soaked in liquid and allowed to expand. Once properly prepared, you can sprinkle them on top of almost anything!

2. Pumpkin Seeds

   Pumpkin seeds work great for a tasty and easy snack and can also be added to salads, yogurt, and soups. They pack a lot of great nutrients like Vitamins C, E, and K, omega-3 fatty acids, and iron in a small package.

3. Almonds

   Commonly considered nuts, almonds are more accurately categorized as a fruit of the almond tree. They are wonderful sources of fiber, protein, magnesium, phosphorus, calcium, potassium, iron, and B vitamins. Like soybeans, they are often used in dairy substitutes and they have been shown to lower cholesterol, strengthen bones, and promote a healthy cardiovascular system. Plus, they are great for your skin and hair!

4. Flaxseeds

Flaxseeds are great additives to plant-based meals. They can be ground up and added to smoothies, oatmeal, cereal, or baked into muffins, bread, and cookies. They are high in protein, magnesium, zinc, and B vitamins. They also aid in digestion and help with weight loss by suppressing appetite.

5. Walnuts
These nuts are some of the best natural sources of omega-3 fatty acids. They also contain plenty of vitamin E, protein, calcium, zinc, and potassium. These, like many of the other nuts and seeds on this list, can be enjoyed alone as a snack or added to other dishes.

6. Sesame Seeds
Sesame seeds are a great natural way to lower cholesterol and high blood pressure and can also help with afflictions like migraines, arthritis, and asthma. They are great in bread and crackers and can be used in stir-fry meals and salads.

7. Sunflower Seeds
These seeds are great for vitamin E and contain healthy fats, B vitamins, and iron. They can be eaten dry and are also used to make butter, a great alternative to dairy.

8. Cashews
Though cashews, like almonds, are not technically nuts and are rather the fruit of the cashew tree, they are most commonly treated as nuts. With their low sodium content and great flavor, they are a popular source of protein and vitamins.

9. Brazil Nuts
These delicious nuts from the Bertholletia excelsa tree mature inside a large coconut-like shell. They are wonderful for protein, fiber, iron, and many B-complex vitamins.

10. Pine Nuts

    Pine nuts contain great antioxidants as well as lots of iron, magnesium, and potassium. They are low in calories and go wonderfully with many dishes. You can use them in baked foods or add them in sauces like an Italian pesto.

Whole Grains

1. Quinoa

    Quinoa certainly has made a splash onto the health food scene with countless people boasting about its beneficial qualities. Although it is actually a seed, we treat it mainly as a grain in the way in which it is prepared. This South American gem has an incredible amount of protein and omega-3 fatty acids and is an important staple of anyone looking to get more of these nutrients within a plant-based diet. It can be used in a multitude of dishes and is as versatile as it is healthy!

2. Wheat

    A classic staple, whole wheat is incredibly beneficial to your health. Each serving of whole grain has about 2 to 3 grams of fiber which is a great way to make sure your body is functioning healthily and properly. Be sure to steer clear of multi-grain, however, and go for the stuff marked 100% whole grain to make sure you are getting exactly what you need!

3. Oats

    These whole grains are packed full of heart-healthy antioxidants. Oats are great and can be enjoyed as a fulfilling breakfast in the form of oatmeal and they can also be ground up and used as a healthier flour substitute when baking. Unsweetened oats are the best to buy and if you are craving a little something sugary, throw in a few berries or a dollop of honey if you wish.

4. Brown Rice

    Brown rice is incredibly high in antioxidants and good vitamins. It's relative, white rice is far less beneficial as much of these healthy nutrients get destroyed during the process of milling. You can also opt for red and black rice or wild rice. The meal options for this healthy grain are limitless!

5. Rye

    Rye is an amazing whole grain that contains four times the fiber of regular whole wheat and gives you almost 50% of day-to-day recommended iron intake. When shopping for rye, however, be sure to look for the whole rye marking as a lot of what is on the market is made with refined flour, thus cutting the benefits in half.

6. Barley

    This whole grain is a miracle food for lowering high cholesterol. It can be quick-cooked like oats and serves as a delicious side dish. You can add whatever kind of toppings you desire to give it your own personal flair! Be sure again to seek out the whole-grain barley as other types may have the bran or germ removed.

7. Buckwheat

    Buckwheat is a great gluten-free grain option for those with celiac disease or a gluten intolerance. It's a great source of magnesium and manganese. Buckwheat is used to make delicious gluten free pancakes and easily becomes a morning staple!

8. Bulgur

    This grain is a truly excellent source of iron and magnesium. It also contains a wonderful amount of protein and fiber with one cup containing about 75% of daily recommended fiber and 25% or daily recommended protein. It goes great in salads and soups and is easy to cook. Talk about amazing!

9. Couscous

    This grain is another great source of fiber. A lot of the couscous you see in the store will be made from refined flour, though, so it is important that you seek out the whole wheat kind so that you can get all the healthy, yummy benefits.

10. Corn

    Whole corn is a fantastic source of phosphorus, magnesium, and B vitamins. It also promotes healthy digestion and contains heart-healthy antioxidants. It is important to seek out organic corn in order to bypass all of the genetically modified product that is out on the market.

Fruits

1. Avocado

   Widely acknowledged as an incredibly beneficial and healthy super-fruit, avocados truly are miracle fruits. They are the best way possible to get the kind of substantial serving of healthy monounsaturated fatty acids that many people subscribing to a plant-based diet seek to supplement. They also contain about 20 different vitamins and minerals and are packed with important nutrients. On top of that, they taste amazing and go well with almost any dish, breakfast, lunch, or dinner!

2. Grapefruit

   Grapefruits are packed full of Vitamin C, containing much more than oranges. Half a grapefruit provides you with almost 50% of your recommended daily vitamin C. It also gives you incredible levels of Vitamin A, fiber, and potassium. It can help with afflictions like arthritis and is a great remedy for oily skin.

3. Pineapple

   This fruit can be prepared and enjoyed in a variety of ways making it not only a tasty and fun treat but also a great healthy choice! It is full of anti-inflammatory nutrients that can help reduce the risk of stroke or heart attack. Some studies show that it also increases fertility.

4. Blueberries

These little berries not only taste delicious and go with so many different dishes, they are also full of vitamin C and healthful antioxidants. Studies also show that it promotes eye health and can slow macular degeneration which causes older adults to go blind.

5. Pomegranate

    Whether in juice form or seed, consuming pomegranate is a great way to get potassium. It has fantastic antioxidants (three times more than green tea or red wine) that work to promote cardiovascular and heart health as well as lower cholesterol levels

6. Apple

    The old saying "an apple a day keeps the doctor away" is not just an old wives' tale! It is low-calorie and incredibly healthy. Apples contain antioxidants that protect brain cell health and are heart-healthy. They can also lower high cholesterol and aid in weight loss and healthy teeth.

7. Kiwi

    This tart, delicious fruit is not only unique but also full of great vitamins like C and E. These are powerful antioxidants that some studies show help with eye health and can even lower chances of cancer. They are low-calorie and very high in fiber. This makes them great for aiding in weight loss and they make a wonderful, quick, easy, and guilt-free snack.

8. Mango

    Mangoes have excellent levels of the nutrient beta-carotene. The body converts this into Vitamin A which in turn strengthens bone health and the immune system. They also have a huge amount of Vitamin C- 50% of the daily recommended value to be exact.

9. Lemons

    Everyone knows that lemons and other citrus fruit are high in Vitamin C, however, they are also an excellent source of antioxidants, fiber, and folate. Lemons can help lower cholesterol, the risk of some kinds of cancer, and blood pressure. All at just 17 calories a serving!

10. Cranberries

    Cranberries are another fruit that have more than one health benefit. They have great vitamin C and fiber levels and have more antioxidants than many other fruits and vegetables. At only 45 calories a serving, it is a great way to boost your immune system, keep your urinary tract healthy, and absorb other important nutrients like Vitamins E, K, and manganese.

Armed with these plant food MVPs, you can begin to make your transition into a healthy, delicious plant-based diet. Incorporating these foods into your diet will help you build balanced meals that will give you the energy and sustenance you need to go about your day. All of these top ten MVPs are incredibly healthy so you can indulge in them guilt-free because you know that they are giving you so many valuable vitamins, minerals, antioxidants, and other nutrients. Many of these foods are low in calories as well and have amazing health benefits like lowering high cholesterol and promoting a healthy heart and cardiovascular system. If you keep these MVPs in mind, you really cannot go wrong. And as a bonus, there is so much room for creative meal opportunities that are bursting not only with flavor but also with amazing health benefits.

So, how do you transition into a plant-based diet? The easy answer is gradually. Remember, slow and steady always wins the race, every time. Though it is positive, there is no diminishing the fact that this will be a big change for you, especially if you have become used to consuming a lot of animal products and processed foods. Things may feel different and unfamiliar at first, so it is natural to be hesitant. But in reality, transitioning into a plant-based diet is not a scary thing. You can start small! Begin by slowly adding more vegetables, beans, fruits, whole grains, seeds, and nuts to your diet. Here are a few suggestions:

- Make a grocery list that incorporates at least two items from each of our four MVP lists mentioned above. Lists are a great way to get motivated and stay on task; color coordination never goes astray either. Make the list aesthetically appealing or even turn it into a chart and start tracking what items you've tried, liked and will repurchase and what items you'll try next grocery shop.

- Slowly start clearing out your pantry, cupboards and fridge of processed, unhealthy foods so you aren't tempted to snack on them when at home and replace them with healthy substitutes (below we will discuss some fantastic alternatives). You may keep one or two indulgences to begin with as you slowly wean yourself off sweets and retrain your mind.
- Try to incorporate two or three of our MVPs into your dinner each night even if it's a small proportion to begin with. You might start with these foods as a side dish and slowly build up to surrounding your meals around them. You could begin the transition with MVP Mondays and make a delicious meal especially on these nights packed with valuable nutrients – a good way to start the week!
- Try something different for dessert! If you must snack after dinner try some fruits as they are sure to satisfy your sugar cravings, have some blueberries, pomegranates or strawberries with some delicious coconut yoghurt.
- Make your lunch for work, either the night before (or morning of if you have time) and restrict yourself to only buying lunch once a week as a treat. This will enable you to understand exactly what's going into your body and eliminate the need to play that guessing game: *what exactly was in the mysterious lasagna from the café?!*
- Start taking little containers to work full of nuts or cut up fruit and leaving them on your desk or in your bag to pick at whenever you feel a little hungry. This is a great way to train your mind to stop thinking 'snack' means junk food, it doesn't have to and I ensure you your energy levels will rise.

This will help you get familiar with plant-based food products and start to make them a staple in your day to day consumptions. Slowly but surely the sugar cravings will diminish as you cleanse your body with whole foods. Tailor your plant-based choices to your specific likes, but don't be afraid to be a little adventurous and try something new! There are so many wonderful and exciting plant-based foods to try. If you browse your local health food market, it is inevitable that you will come across something you have not yet consumed. Make a little pact with yourself that you will try a new plant-based food every week or every two weeks. See what works for you. You never know, you may just discover your new favorite food!

Once you get used to cooking with more plant-based food products, you can begin cutting back on some of your usual animal products that you consume. That is, of course, if you want to take your plant-based diet that far and make a commitment to not eat as much or any animal products. Either choice is fine. It really depends on what you want and what you are looking to get out of a plant-based diet. If you are looking to cut back on animal products, all forms of red meat and pork should be one of the first things you cut. Too much red meat in anyone's diet is not a good thing, it is just a wise health choice to cut it out. If you are looking to follow a semi-vegetarian diet, turkey can be a great substitute for red meat. Instead of eating a beef hamburger or a pork sausage, try a turkey burger made from ground turkey meat or a turkey sausage. If you are looking to follow a vegetarian or vegan diet, give a veggie burger or lentil burger a try! Many veggie burgers are made with condensed beans and taste amazing. Make your transition gradually and don't make yourself feel guilty if you are craving animal products. It's only natural! Your body has become accustomed to consuming a certain kind of food, so of course, any kind of change will take it by surprise. There are many options out there that act as meat substitutes and so many wonderful vegetarian products. Seitan, tempeh, and tofu are just a few. You may find eating more whole grains like quinoa to be helpful as well because they will fill you up and satisfy cravings.

    If you are looking to cut out dairy, there are countless plant-based alternatives you can reach for that will give you great calcium and vitamin D. Soy milk, almond milk, rice milk, and nut milk are just a few options. Be sure that you read the nutrition facts and labels carefully so that you know exactly how much of your daily recommended vitamin D and calcium you are getting per serving. Coconut milk also makes a great dairy substitute and goes fantastically with a morning cup of coffee or tea. Its creaminess and rich flavor make it so much more tantalizing than regular whole milk. Coconut milk can also be used in the place of cream in other places as well. If you are looking to make a thick and creamy soup, look no further than coconut milk! Instead of butter, reach for cashew or almond butter instead. There are also many types of vegan butter substitute products out there on the market. A trip to your local health food store will present you with a multitude of tasty, healthy options. You also do not have to say goodbye to yogurt if you make the switch away from dairy. You can find delicious types of almond or coconut yogurt and can garnish them with whatever kind of fruit or granola you desire. Plant-based yogurt makes a great alternative to your Greek yogurt. If you are craving ice cream, try using bananas and coconut milk to make your own homemade ice cream! Your options within a plant-based diet are truly as limitless as your imagination is. There are so many things to try and foods to discover. Use the building blocks of the top ten fruits, nuts, veggies, and whole grains and go on from there! Every meal can be a new adventure while you transition into a plant-based diet. If you find yourself craving foods that don't adhere to your new chosen diet, remind yourself why you chose to follow a plant-based diet in the first place. You want to feel and look better and live a healthier lifestyle where you have more energy and passion to do the things you want to do. All of that processed food is slowing you down and eating this more holistic, healthful food will get you closer towards your ultimate goal of living your best possible life. Remember that this kind of life will make you feel so much better than a momentary indulgence of unhealthy food. It is also important that you do not set yourself up for failure. Make realistic goals for yourself. This diet change, like most changes in life, is more likely going to become a permanent lifestyle change than a quick fix that you give up a week or a month down the track, if you start small and gradual. If you begin by cutting out just a few things here and adding a few things there and gradually build up as the weeks go by, you will find yourself being so much more successful than you would be if you just made a sudden, drastic change. And if you do deviate from your diet either purposefully or by accident, don't beat yourself up about it. Just pick up and keep working towards your goal of living a healthy, clean, plant-based, whole food lifestyle.

CHAPTER 3 – The Benefits

One of the main reasons that urge people to switch to a plant-based diet is the fact that it has so many wonderful and amazing health benefits. When you cut out all of the bad, processed food from your diet and replace it instead with whole, unrefined, and carefully-sourced plant products, you feel the benefits almost immediately. In fact, the healthy change is really what keeps most people on the diet. There is so much motivation to stay within the parameters of a plant-based diet when you are actually feeling better, healthier, and have more energy and stamina. Who would want to go back to eating unhealthily and feeling slow and sluggish after getting a taste of what your life on plant-based foods is like? And as an added bonus, you can set your conscience at ease and know that you are taking the steps towards making a better, more protected planet. The plant-based diet is without a doubt one of the most environmental ways of eating you could choose.

There is no denying that we are in the midst of a crisis of chronic diseases like high cholesterol, diabetes, and high-blood pressure. Many people blame the almost universal shift to eating foods that are processed and animal-sourced like refined grains, sugar, salt, meat, oil, dairy, soda, and eggs. Most of the time, these foods are high in fat and low in nutritional value but we keep reaching for them all the same. However, there most certainly is hope. Plant-based diets are becoming much more mainstream and popular amongst people looking to improve their health and lengthen their lifespans. There are so much more products on the market geared towards helping people achieve a healthy, plant-based diet lifestyle than there used to be. Nowadays, you can easily find entire restaurants devoted to serving healthy plant-based meals and health food stores are a dime a dozen. It is easier than ever to switch to a plant-based diet. And that most certainly is good news for you.

We know for a fact that a plant-based diet is a healthier choice than eating lots of processed foods and animal products. Extensive research has been done on this topic. In one study, researchers used vegetarians who had lapsed from their diets as their main focus group. They found that people who used to subscribe to a vegetarian diet but fell out of it and began to eat meat at least once a week experienced an extremely raised risk of heart disease, stroke, diabetes, and weight gain. Studying them for 12 years after they transitioned away from a vegetarian diet, researchers found that life-expectancy was decreased as well. In studies where researchers put certain groups afflicted with diseases like heart disease, high cholesterol, or high blood pressure on an interventional plant-based diet, they found significant increases in satisfaction and health. These groups placed on plant-based diets reported that they were happier with their diet, had increased energy, better digestion, improved sleep, and overall better general and mental health. A plant-based diet has been proven to lower body weight, reduce sugar levels, and aids the body in controlling cholesterol levels. It also helps deal with your emotional and mental health. Many people who switch to a plant based diet claim to experience a lessening of afflictions such as anxiety, fatigue, and depression. It gives many a greater sense of well-being and makes day-to-day functioning easier and more enjoyable.

Because switching to a plant-based diet increases your intake of potassium-rich foods, most people experience lower blood-pressure almost automatically. Whole grains, nuts, seeds, legumes, and fruits and vegetables all contain a great deal of potassium which directly targets blood pressure and lowers it while a lot of meats and animal products lack potassium and can actually pose the risk of raising cholesterol and blood pressure. These good plant foods also contain great amounts of vitamin B6 which helps lower blood pressure as well. With lower blood pressure comes decreased stress and anxiety. It's a win-win! And since blood pressure and cholesterol tend to be tandem, symbiotic issues, it is important to note that plants do not contain any cholesterol. Therefore, a plant-based diet is a kind of foolproof way to lower your cholesterol. High cholesterol and blood pressure are dangerous factors that lead to heart disease, the number one killer of adults in the United States. A plant-based diet thus lowers your risk of heart disease because it ensures that you are putting better, healthier foods into your body that will not make your blood pressure and cholesterol levels sky rocket like some of the other fatty, processed foods and animal products out there.

Followers of a plant-based diet also experience better blood sugar levels. The simplest way to combat high blood sugar is to consume more fiber as is slows the absorption of sugar into the bloodstream. Plant foods and whole grains are incredibly high in fiber while animal products have been proven to raise blood sugar to unhealthy and at times dangerous levels. More balanced blood sugar helps prevent against type 2 diabetes and results in a much healthier life. Whole foods that are nutritious and low in fat also greatly decrease your risk of cancer. Some animal products such as cured meats are thought to be linked to the development of certain cancers. With a plant-based diet, your chances of having cancer are much lowered than someone who does not subscribe to a plant-based diet. It is for these many reasons that many doctors actually champion the plant-based diet and recommend it to patients who are overweight or afflicted with high cholesterol, high blood pressure, or other cardiovascular troubles. Plant-based diets have been shown time and time again to be economical and low-risk ways to make a significant change in one's health for the better. Switching to a plant-based diet may help lower the body mass index (BMI) in addition to blood pressure and cholesterol levels. Because of this, patients may need to take less medications in order to treat their illnesses, thus cutting out unnecessary expenses and the need to take many pills. All of these heart healthy benefits also manifest themselves in the form of weight management and appetite control, all of which we will delve further into in the next chapter.

When you begin to feel immensely healthier due to all the benefits of a plant-based diet, it is inevitable that your mental and emotional health will follow along. Many people notice improved sleeping patterns after making the switch. Not only do they sleep more regularly, the sleep deeper and better. Sleep is so important to our mental and physical health and unfortunately, it is usually one of the first things we sacrifice in our daily lives. There are deadlines to be met, tasks to be completed, and things to do- it can all get overwhelming. When do we have time to sleep? And when we do, is it a good sleep? Switching to a plant-based diet can really help you get in control of your sleep and maximize the actual benefits of your pillow time. Eating plant-based makes the body a well-oiled machine and as such, it becomes more able to recharge itself efficiently. Therefore, you get the most out of your precious, valuable time for sleep. Better sleep can lead to a significant increase in the quality of one's mental health. A good night's sleep elevates mood and boosts energy so that you can be more productive and motivated during the day.

In addition to the many medical benefits of switching to a plant-based diet, there are also some truly powerful and indisputable cosmetic benefits as well. Many studies have shown that there is a significant and strong link between the consumption of dairy products like milk, butter, or cheese, and undesirable skin conditions like acne, eczema, and early signs of aging. Milk contains many similar properties to the hormone testosterone due to other hormones like progesterone making their way into the milk. It is thought that these hormones stimulate the oil glands of the skin, especially the face. An excess of sebum, or oil, is produced and thus acne occurs. This excess oil clogs your pores and can lead to other troublesome skin blemishes such as blackheads and whiteheads. This continuous cycle of clogged pores, blemishes, and acne takes a lot out of your skin and can cause scarring and stress. This can lead to signs of premature aging and skin loses its elasticity and vitality. Many people who switch to a plant-based diet notice an incredibly rapid improvement in the condition of their skin. People who have suffered from acne and started eating plant-based foods have noticed their skin clear significantly. This is in no way by chance. Cutting out or greatly reducing dairy can really help give your skin a new lease on life. If you are struggling with acne and have tried nearly everything under the sun such as harsh chemicals, expensive facials and skin treatments, or countless different brands claiming to heal your skin problems, something as simple as a plant-based diet may be the answer you've been searching for.

Followers of a plant-based diet have also raved about the excellent anti-aging benefits of the diet. Collagen, something our bodies naturally produce in abundance when we are young, is the key factor of what makes skin supple, resilient, firm, and have elasticity. As we get older, collagen production slows and our skin suffers as a result, becoming prone to sagginess and thinness. While this is a natural and inevitable part of life, collagen loss does not have to be so drastic as we age. A plant-based diet has been proven to boost collagen in your body by providing all of the important nutrients and amino acids that make up collagen and how it is produced. In a sense, subscribing to a plant-based diet is kind of like taking a dip in the fountain of youth! Fruits and vegetables like kale, broccoli, asparagus, spinach, grapefruit, lemons, and oranges are chock-full of vitamin C which is an extremely important component in producing the amino acids that make up collagen. The kind of lean protein found in nuts is important in keeping collagen around, adding to skin cell longevity and resilience. Red vegetables like tomatoes, beets, and red peppers all contain lycopene which is a kind of antioxidant that protects skin from the sun while simultaneously increases collagen production. Foods rich in zinc such as certain seeds and whole grains also promote collagen because the mineral repairs damaged cells and reduces inflammation. So many of the plant-based staples contain incredible amounts of all these collagen-boosting nutrients that you do not even have to go out of your way to seek them out. It is all right there in front of you! Looking and feeling younger has never been so easy. It really does start with the internal to make the external radiant and glowing, outer beauty starts from within.

In short, there are no two ways about it - switching to a plant based diet is good for your heart, your health, your mind, and even your physical appearance! The facts of the matter are undeniable. Plant foods contain so many of the incredibly good nutrients that our bodies need to function properly. Making these foods a priority and centering your meals around them rather than just eating vegetables as an occasional side dish or a piece of fruit every now and then makes a huge difference in your health. By eating a diet heavy on meat, dairy, and other animal products and processed foods, it is easy to miss out on the wonderfully beneficial vitamins, minerals, antioxidants, and other nutrients that are in fruits, vegetables, legumes, tubers, grains, nuts, and seeds. Switching to a plant-based diet gives you the opportunity to obtain all of these healthful ingredients that will without a doubt lead you to a better, more fulfilling life.

CHAPTER 4 – Weight Loss

In line with the many health benefits gained from embarking upon a plant-based diet, so many people have found true and lasting success in weight loss. In the United States, obesity is a rampant and dangerous epidemic that many suffer from. With all the processed, unhealthy foods on the market and the concept of valuing meat and other animal products over plant-based foods, it is no wonder. Not many people who do not follow a plant-based diet know just how beneficial a shift in diet could be for them if they find themselves struggling with weight. Sure, there are plenty of fad diets out there that may help you lose weight fast if you have a special occasion coming up or are simply tired and frustrated of being overweight. However, these fad diets do not truly work in the long run because they are not sustainable. You will always end up gaining the weight back and as a result, you will become even more frustrated and discouraged. As we have discussed before, the processed food diet is a never ending, vicious cycle. On top of that, many fad diets are incredibly risky, dangerous, and detrimental to your health. Many people believe that the only way to lose unwanted weight is to drastically cut calories and lower your intake of food in general. This method, however, dangerously depletes your body of essential nutrients. If you are performing rigorous exercise at the same time, the results could be catastrophic and not nearly close to worth the pain. Instead of making desperate attempts to lose weight that will inevitably end in failure, you should make the change to a plant-based diet instead.

Plant-based eating is safe, healthy, and will make you feel great. Once you transition into eating mostly plant-based foods, you will find that your cravings for junk food will be significantly reduced and you will actually start to crave the healthier foods you have begun introducing into your diet. You do not have to meticulously and painstakingly count calories on a plant-based diet. You simply have to create well-rounded, healthy meals full of the protein, vitamins, and minerals you require to get through your day. Many of the ingredients in plant-based dishes are naturally low in calories anyway so it's not even something that has to be on your radar.

In one study, researchers looked at a group of about thirty people and put them on a plant-based diet regimen. They were told to eat as much as they wanted but they had to make sure that it fell within the parameters of the low-fat and plant-based rubric they gave them. They emphasized legumes, vegetables, fruits, whole grains, nuts, and seeds and were allowed different starches like bread, pasta, and potatoes. These starches greatly help with satiation and make you feel full and nourished. Refined oils, animal products, and fatty, highly-processed foods were discouraged by the researchers and the participants had to cut back on sugar and salt. After a year of studying the participants and tracking their individual journeys, the researchers found that on average, the participants lost and kept off around 25 pounds and cut 3 and a half inches from their waistlines. That is an incredible and significant amount of progress, especially for people who have struggled with losing weight and maintaining a healthy body mass index. Because of this and countless other success stories, the plant-based diet has been touted by many health experts and nutritionists. It simply is the best way to make a significant change in weight management in a healthy, safe, and productive way.

Many followers of a plant-based diet find that the foods they consume help with appetite control and suppression. This is largely due to the fact that so many plant-based foods, especially whole grains, are naturally high in fiber and fill you up. Over-eating ceases to be a problem when you are consuming such healthy, satisfying foods. They do not give you a false sense of feeling full either. They really, truly fill you up and give you the nourishment your body needs. Healthy plant-based foods boost your metabolism and set your body on track for smooth, steady weight loss. For example, simple bell peppers have amazing capabilities. They contain dihydrocapsiate which is an incredible, metabolism-boosting compound and an incredible amount of vitamin C. This is important because vitamin C counteracts the stress hormones that cause you to store fat, especially around the midsection. Just one cup of these peppers allots you up to three times your daily dose of vitamin C. Add that to the increased metabolism they create and you have a recipe for weight-loss super food. And it's not just bell peppers. There are so many fruits and veggies that contain valuable amounts of vitamin C and metabolism-boosting capabilities. Onions contain quercetin, a nutrient that promotes blood flow and helps your body naturally regulate glucose levels, thus burning stored fat and preventing new fat cells from forming on your body. They are also incredibly beneficial to your cardiovascular health. Spinach is full of protein and aids in muscle recovery and growth, boosting your metabolism. With so many options for easy weight loss foods out there, it's time you take the bull by the horns and really start taking advantage of them!

Time and time again, plant-based diets have been found by researchers, doctors, scientists, and health experts to be the most effective and sustainable way to lose weight and keep it off. A plant-based diet lets you eat freely and healthily. You do not have to stress over every calorie you consume. You do not have to track every dietary move you make. All you have to do is stick to plant-based foods and stay away from over-processed, refined foods. The more accustomed you become to eating a plant-based diet, the more you keep craving those delicious veggies, grains, fruits, and nuts! Instead of being trapped in a frustrating and demoralizing cycle of trying to lose weight unsuccessfully, now you can find yourself comfortably placed in a routine of making healthy choices and watching the pounds melt away.

CHAPTER 5 – Concerns

Having gone over the many benefits of switching to a plant-based diet, it is only right that we address some concerns that you may have about making plant foods the most important part of your diet. It is, after all, a big lifestyle change and a plant-based diet will only impact your health positively if you go into it thoughtfully, safely, and armed with as much information as possible. Only then will you be able to create balanced, healthy meals for yourself. Given all of the amazing healthy aspects of a plant-based diet, there is not a doubt that you can successfully get all of the nutrients, vitamins, and minerals that you need from your diet. Plants contain all of the things which are essential for our survival. So many people practice a plant-based diet with great success and satisfaction. However, it is easy to fall into the trap of doubting that a plant-based diet is sustainable and will give you all of the essential nutrients your body craves. Meat-eating and the consumption of animal products is, after all, the widely accepted mainstream. So, if you have any worries about whether or not a plant-based diet will work for you, don't panic! A plant-based diet is a safe, healthy choice and here's why.

The most common concern of those who embark upon a plant-based diet have is the question of whether or not they will be able to get essential nutrients such as protein or iron without meat or animal products as the primary staple of their diet. Many people incorrectly believe that a plant-based diet results in a deficiency of protein, iron, calcium, and other important nutrients and vitamins. The truth is, subscribers of a plant based diet have no trouble at all getting the nutrients they need. Plant foods such as soybeans, hemp seed, pumpkin seed, peanuts, seitan, tempeh, tofu, lentils, kidney, navy, black, and lima beans, green peas, almonds, cashews, chickpeas, edamame, and walnuts are all extremely high in protein. And that is just naming a few. There are countless other plant foods that will provide you with the protein you need to live a well-balanced, healthy life. Most of these high-protein foods are also incredibly rich in iron. Legumes like lentils and soybeans, grains such as quinoa and brown rice, nuts and seeds like pumpkin, sunflower, and cashews, vegetables like tomatoes, chard, and collard greens are all excellent sources of iron. On top of that, iron absorption into the body is inhibited by dairy products like cheese, so cutting down on animal products may actually help you get more of the iron you need! For calcium, soy products make an excellent dairy substitute and vegetables like broccoli, kale, collards, okra, and mustard greens will give you what you need.

While it is more than possible to get the nutrients you need through plant foods, it is always a good idea to cover your bases and really ensure that you are giving yourself what your body needs, even for those who choose not to adopt a plant-based diet it is important to provide your body with essential nutrients. Many followers of plant-based diets choose to take a few natural daily supplements like Vitamin B12, (aids in protein metabolism and forming oxygen-transporting blood cells and overall nervous system health), Vitamin D (enhances calcium absorption, boosts immune system), Omega-3 fatty acids (important to brain development), Iodine (aids in thyroid function), Iron, Calcium, or Zinc. You should talk to your doctor or nutritionist and decide which supplements, if any, are right for you based upon what kind of plant-based diet you subscribe to. There are also many physical and virtual communities of people who follow plant-based diets where you can ask for tips and suggestions from others on how to go about approaching supplements and ensuring you are getting all of the essential nutrients you require. The wonderful thing about a plant-based diet is that you have the ability to tailor it to your specific needs and desires.

For many years, we have accepted that the default diet for humans must include meat, dairy, and other various animal products. We are capable of being omnivores so it is no wonder that this way of eating has been widely accepted as indisputable dietary law. However, our prehistoric ancestors were mainly herbivores. They were hunter-gatherers who mainly lived off of fruits, vegetables, nuts, seeds, and legumes that they found scavenging and gathering. Meat was only consumed once in a while as hunting was hard going and we were not the incredibly evolved predators we are today. To our prehistoric ancestors who did not yet have the capabilities of domesticating plant crops and sourcing mass amounts of food, the occasional meat they were able to consume was relatively important to their diet as it provided them with important protein that they might not have been able to find while scavenging and gathering wild plant foods. However, in our day and age, we now have the ability to domesticate crops and are able to produce mass amounts of food. We have the ability to obtain protein-rich vegetables, nuts, seeds, and legumes easily and no longer have that desperate need for meat to supplement our diets. We have evolved past that. As such, meat and animal products are not as vital and paramount in our diets as they used to be. We have developed the capabilities to survive and thrive without them. At the end of the day plants really do contain everything we need!

CHAPTER 6 – Easy, Delicious Recipes

Now that you have all the details and background information on the plant-based diet, it's time to put all your newfound knowledge into action! The world of plant-based cooking is vast and virtually never ending. There are so many different recipes and meals out there for you to try out. If you have been stuck in the meat and dairy grind for most of your life, get ready to broaden your horizons and experience some real flavor and excitement! There is an infinite amount of delicious plant-based dishes that you may have never tried before. So, if you are wondering how to dive in and start making plant-based meals, look no further! In this chapter, you will find three days' worth of easy, manageable plant-based recipes for breakfast, lunch, dinner, and a few snacks in between. Enjoy, and remember, don't be afraid to get creative and try new things!

Day 1

Breakfast

Cinnamon Maple Oatmeal

This recipe is great for a quick breakfast in the morning. It can be prepared on the stovetop or in the microwave, whichever you prefer. This yummy oatmeal will give you the important nutrients and satisfaction you need to get your day started the right way!

Ingredients:

- Oats (0.75 cup)
- Water (1 cup)
- Ground flaxseed (0.5 tbsp)
- Raw maca powder (0.5 tsp)
- Unsweetened almond milk (0.5 cup)
- Ground cinnamon (0.25 tsp)

- Maple syrup (1 tbsp)
- Banana, blueberries, raw nuts for toppings

1. In a bowl (or pot if you are making this on the stove), mix the water, almond milk, and oats together. Microwave for 2 minutes or heat up on the stovetop until mixture bubbles slightly.
2. Once heated, mix in your flaxseed, maca powder, cinnamon, and maple syrup. If you have been cooking your oatmeal on the stove, remove from heat and place into a serving bowl.
3. Add your choice of toppings! Banana, blueberries, and various raw nuts make excellent additions.

Mid-morning snack

1 cup of diced cantaloupe.

Cantaloupe is a melon that is extremely high in potassium B vitamins, vitamin K, magnesium, and fiber. It also serves as a great source of omega-3 fat.

Lunch

Pita pizza

Who says a plant-based diet means cutting out pizza? In this simple lunch recipe, you don't have to say goodbye to a guilty pleasure. You can say hello to a delicious, healthy alternative!

Ingredients

- Marinara sauce (or hummus)
- Large pita
- Vegetables of your choice, i.e. onions, spinach, tomatoes, olives, peppers, mushrooms, etc.
- Protein like tempeh, seitan, tofu, or another plant-based meat substitute
- Vegan cheese

1. Lay out your ingredients and preheat oven to 350 degrees Fahrenheit.
2. Spread a generous layer of marinara sauce or hummus on your large pita.
3. Add desired toppings.
4. Bake in the oven for about 5 or 10 minutes or until all the toppings are sufficiently heated to your liking.

Afternoon Snack

A handful of cashews (about 16 individual cashews)

One of the nut MVPs, cashews, are full of great vitamins, antioxidants, and minerals that all promote healthy bodily functioning.

Dinner

Vegetarian Tacos

These tacos are great for a meal for one or for the whole family! Garnish with some lime and a splash of hot sauce for that extra oomph.

Ingredients

- Several small tortillas
- Canned black beans
- Ground cumin (0.5 tsp)
- Chili powder (0.5 tsp)
- Sliced avocado
- Salsa
- Lettuce
- Tomato
- Chopped cilantro

1. Heat up a stack of small tortillas in the microwave. Tip: Lay a moistened paper towel on top of the stack to lock in freshness and make sure the tortillas do not dry out and get hard or crunchy.
2. Partly drain canned black beans and mash up in a pot. Set the pot on medium heat on the stovetop and add your cumin and chili powder. Continue mashing and stirring the mixture together and let it cook covered for about two minutes to heat up. It is important to keep an eye on the beans and mix as necessary so that they do not stick to the bottom of the pot and burn.
3. Remove the beans from the heat and place servings on individual tortilla. Top tortillas with some sliced avocado, cilantro, lettuce, tomato, and salsa. Add any other toppings or sauces you desire. Vegan cheese works great on these veggie tacos!

Day 2

Breakfast

Banana Muffins

Prepare these the night before for an easy, grab-and-go kind of breakfast. These muffins are packed with fiber and will definitely get you started on the right foot.

Ingredients

- 4 ripe bananas
- Ground flaxseed (2 tbsps)
- Ground cinnamon (1 tsp)
- Vanilla extract (0.5 tbsp)
- Baking powder (0.5 tbsp)
- Baking soda (0.5 tsp)
- Apple cider vinegar (0.5 tbsp)
- Apple sauce (0.5 cup)
- Apple juice (0.5 cup)
- Ground oats (2 cups)

1. Preheat your oven to 350 degrees Fahrenheit
2. For preparation, place cupcake liners in a muffin pan and grind up oats. Run bananas through a food processor or mash up into a fine puree manually. Add in applesauce, juice, and vinegar and blend together thoroughly.
3. Place all of your dry ingredients, including your ground oats into a large bowl and mix well.
4. Combine your banana puree and dry ingredients and mix just enough, being careful not to over-mix.
5. Pour this mixture about two-thirds of the way into your cupcake liners
6. Once the oven is preheated, bake the muffins for 20 to 23 minutes. The tops should be slightly golden brown and not sticky in the center. Once baked, remove from the oven and let cool.

Midmorning Snack

Whole wheat pita slices with a side of hummus.

Nothing beats those mid-morning cravings better than a delicious helping of healthy whole wheat pita and hummus. You can buy store brand or make your own using this great recipe:

Ingredients:

- Cooked chickpeas (2 cups)
- Keep the chickpea liquid and set aside to use later (2 tablespoons worth)
- Garlic cloves (2 large)
- Salt (1 tsp)
- Tahini (one-third cup)
- Lemon juice (8 tbsps)
- Tabasco sauce (a few drops)
- Olive oil (drizzled)
- Paprika (garnish)

1. In a food processor, combine all of the ingredients except for salt, olive oil, and paprika. Process until the mixture is roughly pureed.
2. Add salt little by little, processing, then adding more. Taste as you go to make sure it is neither too salty nor lacking.
3. Once you have salted it to your liking, remove from the processor and place into a container. Drizzle olive oil on top and add a dash of paprika in the container. Will keep for up to five days in a sealed container in the refrigerator.

Lunch

Quesadillas

We're taking the "queso" out of quesadillas here, but they are no less tasty than their cheesy, less healthy alternatives. These make for a great lunch you can enjoy at home or pack up and take to work.

Ingredients

- Organic mashed sweet potatoes (1 can)
- 2 Large tortillas
- Black beans (0.5 cup)
- Chopped green pepper
- Chopped onion

1. Place the mashed sweet potatoes in a microwavable safe bowl and cook it on high for three minutes.
2. Lay out one of your large tortillas and spread the mashed sweet potatoes evenly on top.
3. Add your beans, green pepper, and onion
4. Cover by placing another large tortilla on top.
5. In a large skillet, grill each side of the quesadilla for three minutes. Remove from the heat, cut into quarters, and serve. Add salsa on the side for dipping if desired.

Afternoon Snack

Apple slices and Peanut Butter

This is a foolproof never-failing staple that will always leave you feeling full, satisfied, and wonderfully nourished.

Dinner

Portobello Pot Roast

If you are craving for a savory, oven-baked dinner, then this is the meal for you. This creative take on a pot roast is delectable and hearty while not being overly heavy or overly high in sodium like meat pot roast.

Ingredients

- Sliced Portobello mushrooms (4 large)
- Sliced onion (1 large)
- Pressed garlic (2 cloves)
- White wine (0.5 cup)
- Whole-wheat flour (3 tbsps)
- Sage (1 tsp)
- Rosemary (1 sprig)
- Thyme (4 sprigs)
- Vegan Worcestershire sauce (2 tsps)
- Basil (1 tsp)
- Veggie broth (3 cups)
- Potatoes (4 large)
- Chopped carrots (4 large)
- Salt and pepper to taste

1. Preheat oven to 350 degrees Fahrenheit. Heat 0.25 cups of the white wine in a large pan and add mushroom slices. Let it cook and brown slightly, moving and shifting

ever so often. Once cooked, remove the mushroom slices from the pan and put on a plate to the side.
2. Add the rest of the wine (0.25 cups) to your pan and place the garlic and onion along with it. Let onions caramelize and let them start to brown. Remove the onions and set alongside your mushrooms.
3. In a small bowl, combine the sage, basil, and flour. Mix 0.25 cups of the veggie broth so that a paste is created. Pour this new mixture into the pan you have been using to cook the mushrooms and onions. Being sure to keep stirring constantly, start pouring the remaining veggie broth slowly in order to create a gravy.
4. Once you have added the rest of the broth, let the mixture cook. When it begins to boil, turn off the stovetop heat and add any other seasonings you desire. Add the carrots, potatoes, salt, pepper, and Worcestershire sauce to your gravy. If the vegetables seem like they could dry out, add extra broth as needed.
5. Place the mushrooms and onions back into the mixture and place entire contents of the pan into a large casserole dish or ceramic pot. Lay the thyme and rosemary on top and place the lid on the container. Bake in the oven for about an hour. Once baked, remove and serve.

Day 3

Breakfast

Potato Scramble on Toast or Wrap

This is a great plant-based take on a spicy scrambled breakfast that will have your taste buds jumping and will definitely wake you up! Plus, it makes a wonderful brunch meal.

Ingredients

- Potatoes chopped into about half inch cubes (2 lb)
- Ground allspice (0.25 tsp)
- Chopped cilantro (0.5 cup)
- Yellow mustard (3 tbsps)
- Chopped red onion (1.5 cup)
- Chopped and seeded jalapeno (1.5 tsps)

- Chopped tomatoes (2)
- Lime juice (3 tbsps, about 2 limes)
- Salt
- Hot Sauce (optional)
- Whole grain bread or tortillas

1. In a pan, combine 1 cup of water with the onion, allspice, jalapeno, and mustard. Stir well and simmer on a medium heat, covering the pan. Cook for 5-10 minutes or until the onions are translucent.
2. Place the potatoes in the mixture and season with salt to taste, add another cup of water afterwards. Set heat to high and cover once more, periodically stirring for 5 minutes.
3. Lower heat back to medium and cook covered for about 10 minutes or until the potatoes are sufficiently tender.
4. Remove from the heat and add the lime juice, tomatoes, and cilantro. Enjoy on top of whole grain toast or wrapped in tortillas. Add hot sauce or other condiments/seasonings as desired.

Midmorning Snack

1 cup of frozen red grapes

This is especially great in the summer for a cool and refreshing snack. It's like nature's very own popsicle!

Lunch

Green Salad and Cooked Quinoa

Sometimes, a simple salad on a busy day is the way to go. The quinoa will give you all the protein you need to carry out your day and finish strong. You can prepare a large batch of quinoa at the beginning of the week and use it in salads and other dishes throughout the week.

Ingredients

- Lettuce (1 head)
- Kale (1 cup)
- Cherry tomatoes (0.5 cup, sliced)
- Cucumber (1 large, chopped)
- Quinoa (1 cup)
- Water (2 cups)
- Balsamic vinegar (1.5 tbsps)
- Olive oil (4 tbsps)
- Salt and pepper (1 pinch each)

1. In a pot on the stove, bring 2 cups of water and 1 cup of quinoa to boil. Once boiling, lower heat, cover, and let it simmer until the quinoa is tender and has absorbed most of the liquid. This should take about 15 or 20 minutes. Once cooked, remove from the heat and fluff with a fork.
2. In a large bowl, combine lettuce, kale, tomatoes, cucumber, and your cooked quinoa together.
3. In a separate, smaller bowl, add vinegar and a pinch of salt and pepper. Mix well. Once mixed, add olive oil and mix together.
4. Add vinaigrette to your veggie and quinoa mixture. Toss well and enjoy!

Afternoon Snack

Oatmeal Lemon Cookies

These cookies are easy to make and taste so great, it's hard to believe they're so healthy and good for you! They contain a great helping of oats, fruit, and nuts in every bite.

Ingredients

- Chopped walnuts (0.75 cup)
- Oat flour (1 cup)
- Quick-cooking oats (0.5 cup)

- Rolled oats (1 cup)
- 10 pitted dates
- Applesauce (1 cup)
- Apple cider vinegar (1.5 tsps)
- Cocoa powder (2 tsps)
- Grated lemon zest (2 tbsps., about 2 lemons)
- Baking soda (0.5 tsp)
- Salt (pinch)
- Vanilla powder (1 tsp)

1. Preheat oven to 275 degrees Fahrenheit and line a couple of baking sheets with parchment paper. Place dates in a bowl with hot water and let sit for about 20 minutes. Draining excess water, place dates in a blender and add vinegar and applesauce. Blend and set on the side.
2. In another bowl, stir all oat products, lemon zest, walnuts, vanilla powder, cocoa powder, salt, and baking soda. Add the blended dates and lightly mix.
3. Gently roll small portions of your dough you just made into balls and then flatten. Be careful to not compact the mixture too hard. Place the individual pieces of flattened dough on the baking sheet.
4. Place cookies in the oven for 35 to 45 minutes or until they look browned and crispy. Let it cool and then eat or store for later!

Dinner

Spinach Pasta Puttanesca

This simple pasta dish is great to make for when you have company over and so easy to make in large quantities. Everyone will be happy and satisfied!

Ingredients

- Whole grain pasta (8 ounces)
- Water (0.25 cup)

- Chopped onion (half)
- Diced tomatoes (15-ounce can)
- Canned marinara sauce (half jar)
- Chopped parsley (one-third cup)
- Sliced garlic (3 large cloves)
- Sun-dried tomatoes (0.5 cup)
- Seedless olives (one-third cup)
- Baby spinach (4 cups)

1. Boil a large pot of water and then add your pasta. Cook uncovered for however long the directions on the box indicate.
2. While your pasta is cooking, heat up a large pan and add water and onion. Sauté until the water evaporates and the onions become translucent.
3. In the pan, add your sun-dried tomatoes, spinach, marinara sauce, diced tomatoes, and olives. Stir well and then add parsley and garlic. Combine.
4. Cook your mixture until the spinach wilts slightly.
5. Once the pasta is cooked and drained, add it to the pan and toss together. Combine well and then remove from heat and serve.

And there you have it! Three days' worth of delicious new recipes to try out for yourself. And don't forget, there are thousands more just waiting to be tried! These recipes are all vegan-friendly and contain no animal products in order to demonstrate just how diverse and varied your meals can be. If you choose to not cut out animal products and instead simply reduce them while putting vegetables, fruit, legumes, tubers, nuts, seeds, and whole grains at the forefront, you can most certainly supplement these recipes with the animal products of your choosing. As we have stated before a plant-based diet is what you make it. You have absolute control over how you wish to tailor it to yourself specifically. So, explore your options and find out what works for you!

Conclusion

Well done and congratulations for making it through to the end of this book. I hope you thoroughly enjoyed reading it and have learnt new essential information about how to structure and incorporate a plant-based diet into your day to day lifestyle.

There are so many powerful and persuasive reasons to make a positive change and switch over to a plant-based diet. A plant-based diet will improve your quality of life, give you more energy and vitality, help you lose unwanted body fat, and it may even lengthen your years on this beautiful planet. And as an added bonus, by making the change you will be making a real and significant difference to our planet Earth's future. So much energy and fossil fuels are wasted by sourcing meat and other animal products, transporting them from place to place across miles and miles of road, and processing all of these animal products. On top of that, there is an enormous crisis of animals being treated extremely inhumanely and cruelly. In order to mass produce meat and animal products to meet the enormous demand of the market, many manufacturers put animal comfort and quality of life last and do not make it a priority to treat them in a humane and ethical fashion. There is also an incredible amount of food waste that happens in the production and processing of animal products. Extraordinary amounts of energy and resources are expended and too much gets simply thrown away. By switching to a plant-based diet, you will be greatly decreasing your carbon footprint and ensuring that fewer animals have to suffer at the hands of humans. And isn't that a good feeling?

Considering all the ethical reasons for switching to a plant-based diet, the enormous health benefits and improved quality of life are the icing on an already extremely appealing cake.

Finally, if you found this book useful in any way, a review on Amazon is always appreciated! Good luck and happy eating!